MEASURE IT!

TEMPERATURE

Casey Rand

Heinemann
LIBRARY
Chicago, Illinois

www.heinemannraintree.com
Visit our website to find out more information about Heinemann-Raintree books.

To order:

☎ Phone 888-454-2279

💻 Visit www.heinemannraintree.com to browse our catalog and order online.

Edited by Megan Cotugno, Louise Galpine, and Abby Colich
Designed by Richard Parker
Original illustrations © Darren Lingard 2009
Picture research by Mica Brancic
Originated by Capstone Global Library, Ltd.
Printed and bound in China by CTPS

13 12 11 10
10 9 8 7 6 5 4 3 2

Library of Congress Cataloging-in-Publication Data

Rand, Casey.
  Measuring temperature / Casey Rand.
     p. cm. -- (Measure it!)
  Includes bibliographical references and index.
  ISBN 978-1-4329-3767-6 (hc) -- ISBN 978-1-4329-3773-7 (pb) 1. Temperature measurements--Juvenile literature. I. Title.
  QC271.4.R36 2010
  536'.50287--dc22
                        2009035275

Acknowledgments

The author and publishers are grateful to the following for permission to reproduce copyright material:

Corbis pp. **4** (©Douglas Peebles), **7** (Brand X/©PNC), **14** (©Michael Benson), **17** (©Frank Lane Picture Agency), **27** (Blend Images/© Hill Street Studios); iStockphoto pp. **5** (©Jan Will), **6** (©Elena Korenbaum), **16** (©Chee-Onn Leong), **23** (©Jan Will), **25** (Missing35mm); Photolibary p. **11** (Oxford Scientific (OSF)/©Ted Kinsman); Science Photo Library p. **20** (David Parker); Shutterstock pp. **10** (©Wong Hock Weng), **12** (©Nikolai Pozdeev), **21** (©Olegusk).

Cover photo of thermometer in the snow reproduced with permission from Photolibrary/Comstock (Creatas).

We would like to thank John Pucek for his invaluable help in the preparation of this book.

Every effort has been made to contact copyright holders of any material reproduced in this book. Any omissions will be rectified in subsequent printings if notice is given to the publisher.

Contents

Some words are printed in bold, **like this**. You can find out what they mean by looking in the glossary on page 30.

What Is Temperature?

We know that lava from a volcano is very hot and that snow and ice in Antarctica are very cold. **Temperature** tells us the hotness or coldness of these things.

Why are some things hot?

Heat is a measure of the transfer of energy in **matter**. Matter is what makes up everything around us. When the tiny particles that make up matter have a lot of energy, they move faster. Matter with less energy moves more slowly.

When an object is hot, it has a lot of heat. This means that its matter has a lot of energy. You cannot see this movement. Remember that the particles that make up matter are too tiny to see. But the particles that make up matter are moving very quickly within a hot object.

The matter the lava is made up of has lots of energy. It is very hot!

Why are some things cold?

When an object is cold, it has a small amount of heat. The particles that make up matter do not have much energy. The particles in matter in a cold object are moving more slowly than those in a hot object.

Antarctica is freezing cold. The particles that make up matter here contain very little energy and are moving very slowly. Brrr!

Why Do We Measure Temperature?

Temperature is a measure of the degree of hotness in an object. But why do we need to know how hot something is? Measuring temperature is very important. How do you choose what you will wear when you get dressed in the morning? It mostly has to do with the temperature outside. What if you wore a T-shirt and walked outside to find that it is very cold? Measuring temperature is very important!

Scientists need to measure and control temperature in many types of experiments. Most reactions in scientific experiments would be impossible to control without being able to measure the temperature.

Baking

Did you know that baking and cooking are forms of scientific reactions? Just like in a science laboratory, it is very important to be able to measure temperature in the kitchen. In the process of candy making, exact temperatures for baking need to be known. Sugar molecules need a very specific amount of **heat** to move at the right speed for forming candy. Without temperature measurement, we might not even have candy!

Scientific reactions helped form these baked goods.

Maintaining homeostasis is important for all humans. Too much heat can cause hyperthermia.

Humans

Humans need to keep their bodies at a very specific temperature. **Hyperthermia** is a condition in which the human body is too hot. This can be very dangerous. **Hypothermia** is a condition in which the human body temperature drops below normal. Our bodies work hard to keep our temperature level. This is called **homeostasis**.

How Do We Measure Temperature?

We use two different scales to measure **temperature**: the **Celsius** Scale and the **Fahrenheit** Scale. Temperature in both of these scales is measured in units called **degrees**. The temperature 21 degrees Celsius, for example, is abbreviated 21°C.

Celsius Scale

Swedish astronomer Anders Celsius (1701–1744) developed the Celsius Scale (also known as centigrade) in 1742. It is used throughout most of the world today. This scale is based on 100 parts, or 100 degrees. Anders Celsius created this scale using measurements of water temperature. In the Celsius Scale, 0° is the temperature at which water freezes, and 100° is the temperature at which water boils.

Fahrenheit Scale

The Fahrenheit Scale is used mainly in the United States. German physicist Daniel Gabriel Fahrenheit developed it in the early 1700s. This scale was created using measurements of salt, water, and ice. In this scale, water freezes at 32° and boils at 212°F.

Converting between scales

We can convert a temperature between the Celsius and Fahrenheit Scales using the formula: °C = (°F - 32) x 5/9. We reverse this equation if we need to convert Celsius to Fahrenheit: °F = (°C x 9/5) + 32.

You Do the Math

The hottest temperature ever recorded on Earth was 136°F in Libya on September 13, 1922. Try using the formula
°C = (°F - 32) x 5/9
to convert the temperature to Celsius.

The coldest temperature ever recorded on Earth was -89.2°C in Antarctica in 1983. Can you convert this temperature to Fahrenheit using the formula
°F = (°C x 9/5) + 32?

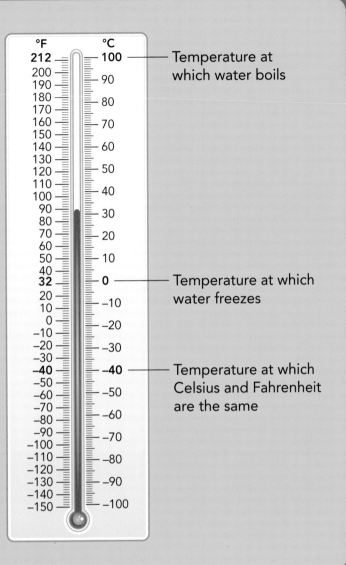

Temperature at which water boils

Temperature at which water freezes

Temperature at which Celsius and Fahrenheit are the same

Did You Know?
There is only one temperature at which these two scales give the exact same temperature: -40°. At -40° both Celsius and Fahrenheit are the same!

What Is Used to Measure Temperature?

Humans are **endothermic**, meaning warm-blooded. This means we maintain the same body **temperature** even if the temperature around us changes. Normal internal body (inside your body) temperature for humans is around 98.6°F, or 37°C. When we touch an object, it feels either warm or cold to us. Humans can estimate temperature using their sense of touch, but this method is not very accurate.

Nature's thermometer

Crickets, like most insects and some animals, are **ectothermic**, or cold-blooded. A cricket's temperature changes when the temperature of its surroundings change. A cricket's chirp will get faster when it is warmer and slower when it is cooler. This is a fun and easy way to measure temperature. Count the number of cricket chirps in 14 seconds and add 40. This will give you the temperature in **Fahrenheit**.

You can figure out the temperature by listening to a cricket chirp.

Instruments we use to measure temperature

Many instruments we use to measure temperature rely on a substance that changes size or shape in response to changes in temperature. Wood, metal, and most other materials change size when they are heated or cooled. This change is too small to see in many materials. However, the change in other materials is large enough to see, and these materials are often used in instruments created to measure temperature.

Thermal imaging can be used to "see" warm objects even in the dark, like this ice skater.

Thermal vision

Many of the instruments used to measure temperature today depend on computers and sensors. **Thermal imaging** is a method to see variation in temperature even in the dark or through smoke. This can be used by firefighters to identify people trapped in a burning building. It can also be used at night to see animals, humans, or any object that is warmer than its surroundings in the dark.

Thermometers

What do we use to measure the temperature of our bodies, our food, and the air outside? The answer is **thermometers**. Thermometers have been around for hundreds of years and have hundreds of uses. Galileo invented a type of thermometer over 400 years ago!

How do thermometers work?

Thermometers usually consist of a glass bulb filled with a liquid and a long, thin tube that extends from the bulb. As temperature increases, the liquid in the thermometer takes up more space and is pushed up the glass tube. The glass tube is labeled with the Celsius or Fahrenheit scale and the height of the liquid in the tube tells us what temperature is.

The average temperature of a gorilla is 41.4°C.

Spring thermometers

Some thermometers use a spring system instead of a liquid-filled tube. These thermometers look like a clock, but show the temperature instead of the time. The spring is made of a metal that changes size when temperature changes. A hand is connected to the spring. The hand points to the correct temperature when the metal spring changes size.

Rounding measurements

Sometimes temperature measurements need to be very precise. This means our measurement needs to be very exact. Other times temperature measurements do not need to be precise and can be rounded up or down. Numbers ending in 1, 2, 3, or 4 can be rounded down. Numbers ending in 5, 6 7, 8, or 9 can be rounded up. Use the chart below to help you decide which way to round a temperature measurement.

You Do the Math

The average human body temperature is 98.6°F. We can round this number up to the nearest whole **degree**: 99°F.

The average temperature of a gorilla is 41.4°C. What is the temperature of the Gorilla rounded to the nearest degree?

Direction	Number
	9
↑	8
	7
	6
	5
	4
↓	3
	2
	1

What is the temperature in outer space?

The easiest way to measure temperature is to use a thermometer, but how do scientists find the temperature of planets in outer space? To measure the temperature on Mars, Venus, and the moon, scientists have been able to use spacecrafts. These spacecrafts have electronics that measure temperatures where they land, much like we would on Earth.

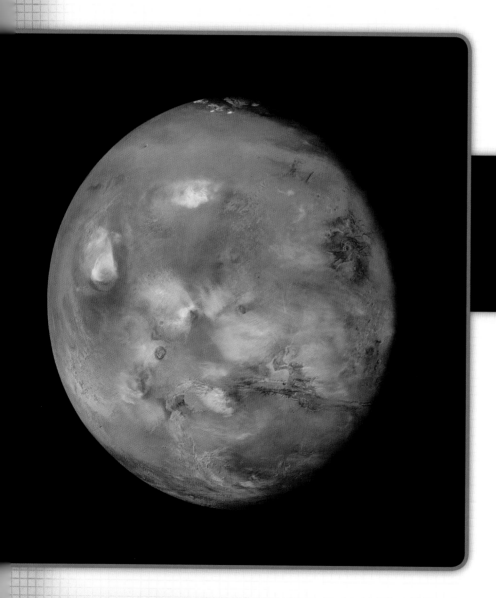

The temperature on Mars is very cold at night. Ice caps from carbon dioxide form on Mars.

Hot topics

The sun is very hot! The sun can heat the Earth from more than 150 million kilometers (92 million miles) away! The center of the sun is estimated to be 15,000,000°C. Scientists can estimate the temperature of the sun by looking at the colors the sun emits. Scientists also have to estimate the temperature of planets that are farther away than Mars and Venus.

Mission to Mars

The temperature on Mars changes a lot every day. The daytime temperature could be 27°C (80°F). At night the temperature can dip to -123°C (-190°F). Imagine you were planning a trip to Mars and wanted to find the daily temperature. If we measured the temperature only once, we might think that Mars is always very cold (if we only measured at night) or always very hot (if we only measured in the day). Sometimes in science we need to make multiple measurements to make sure we find the best answer.

You Do the Math

The table shows the recorded temperature on Mars measured every six hours throughout the day. Can you determine what the average daily temperature of Mars is? Find the average by adding all four temperatures and divide by the number of temperatures you added.

Time	Temperature (°C)
midnight	-70
6:00 a.m.	-30
noon	15
6:00 p.m.	-15

Can Plants and Animals Measure Temperature?

We have seen the many reasons it is important for humans to be able to measure **temperature**. Do plants and animals need to be able to measure temperature, too? How do plants and animals measure temperature?

Plant thermometers

It is very important for plants to be able to measure temperature. Many plants are extremely sensitive to changes in the air around them. Scientists have recently discovered that some plants detect changes in temperature and changes in light to know when they should get ready for winter. That's right! Plants get ready for winter just like animals. Scientists don't know for sure how plants sense temperature, but with young scientists like you studying temperature, we will know one day.

The trees are getting ready for winter. Like other plants and animals, they can sense changing seasons.

This pit viper has heat sensors above its eye to hunt for food.

Animal thermometers

Animals have lots of ways to sense changes in temperature. Many dogs and cats will grow thick hair when the temperatures get cold in the fall. They shed this hair when the temperature gets warmer in the spring. This helps them stay comfortable in the colder and warmer seasons. Iguanas are able to detect temperature in sand as accurately as within about 1°C (2°F). This is important because an iguana's eggs, for example, must be kept at a very particular temperature.

Heat hunters

Many animals use temperature to help them find food. Some snakes have **heat** sensors between their eyes and nostrils that can sense tiny changes in heat even less than 1°C. This helps the snake, like the viper pictured above, identify and find warm food.

How Does Weather Affect Temperature?

Warm summer days can be perfect for playing games, going swimming, and eating ice cream. Colder winter days can be perfect for sledding and building snow people. Which season do you prefer?

The reason for the seasons

Did you know that the Earth is slightly tilted? When the area north of the **equator**, the northern **hemisphere**, is closer to the sun, it gets more sunlight. During this time, it is summer in the northern hemisphere and winter in the southern hemisphere. Six months later, the Earth has revolved halfway around the sun. The southern hemisphere is now closer to the sun, making it summer there and winter in the northern hemisphere.

Measuring temperature throughout the year

Measuring the **temperature** outside is as easy as using a **thermometer**. However, sometimes it may feel warmer or colder outside than the thermometer says. Because of this, two special scales have been created to help us measure how warm or cold it *feels* outside.

The heat index

The **heat index** is a measure of both the temperature and **humidity**. Humidity is a measure of how much **water vapor** is in the air. Humidity can make the air feel even warmer than the temperature alone. The heat index tells us how warm it actually feels outside.

Wind chill

Sometimes wind causes the temperature to feel colder than when the wind is calm. This is called the **wind chill factor**. Scientists use the wind chill factor and the temperature to measure how cold it really feels outside.

This map shows wind direction. Scientists study wind to measure how cold it will feel outside.

Did You Know?
Our body uses sweat as a cooling mechanism. When we sweat, the water on our skin evaporates, helping us to stay cool. The reason humidity can make us feel even hotter on a warm day is that the sweat does not evaporate as efficiently and our body loses one of its cooling mechanisms.

Predicting future temperatures

Meteorologists are a type of scientist that study weather and predict future weather and temperatures. How do meteorologists know what the temperature is going to be in the future? Two times every day weather balloons are launched all across the world at the same time. They fly over 32 kilometers (20 miles) into the sky and measure temperature, wind speed, and other data. Meteorologists can use all of this information to help them predict future temperature.

Predicting weather at home

Even without your own weather balloon, there are lots of ways you can predict weather at home. Feel the morning grass for dew at sunrise. Dew usually indicates that it will not rain today. Dry grass indicates wind and clouds, which could mean rain. Watch the birds. Birds flying high usually mean good weather. Birds fly low when storm fronts are in the area.

Weather balloons make weather measurements and relay them back to meteorologists.

How can we predict temperatures from the past?

Written records from long ago give us a good idea of how weather was in the past. Scientists can speculate what weather may have been like in **prehistoric** times by looking at coral growth, tree sizes, sediments found in rock, and even by investigating ice blocks that have been around for thousands of years.

You Do the Math

Tree rings help scientists determine what temperatures were like hundreds of years ago. Trees form rings in their trunks as they grow. Each ring represents one year of the tree's life. Generally, in cooler climates, these rings grow wider during warmer years. Scientists have learned to estimate temperatures by looking at these rings in very old trees. Can you guess which rings are from the warmest years?

outer ring

middle ring

inner ring

Many trees will grow faster when the temperature is warmer. Wide spaces between the rings means the tree grew a lot that year.

What Is Climate Change?

Climate change is a change in long-term weather patterns. Scientists can use information about past **temperatures** to measure climate change over decades, centuries, and even longer periods of time.

Temperature records

A **temperature record** is a way to show changes in temperature over time. Look at the temperature record below. Can you see any trends in temperature changes over the last 100 years? These long-term changes in weather, even when small, are considered climate change and can be very dangerous for inhabitants of Earth.

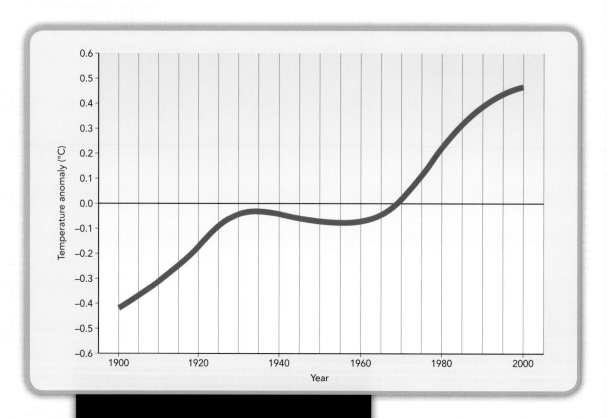

This chart shows temperature records from the 1900s.

Global warming is already having many effects, including melting ice caps, which causes many animals to lose their homes.

Did You Know?
Using temperature records, scientists have determined that we are in a period of **global warming**. Many scientists believe that these increasing temperatures are caused by **greenhouse gases**. These are gases in the atmosphere that absorb and trap **heat**.

Possible causes of greenhouse gases and global warming include: exhaust from automobiles; heating, cooling, and electricity systems; and deforestation (cutting down trees and not planting new ones).

The Earth needs your help!

Global warming is causing sea levels to rise as giant mountains of ice near the north and south poles melt. This is causing flooding in many places and some animals and people are already losing their homes. Global warming has also caused extreme weather changes including hurricanes, droughts, storms, and floods. If we don't do something soon, things will only get worse. There are many things you can do to help stop global warming:

- plant a tree
- use less electricity by turning off lights, TVs, and computers whenever possible
- ride your bike or walk instead of riding in a car
- recycle.

How Does Temperature Affect Things Around Us?

We know **temperature** can make certain materials expand or contract. We also know temperature can make us feel hot or cold. Temperature is a powerful force. It can also change the way materials look and feel.

States of matter

There are three main **states of matter**:

- solids: such as ice cubes
- liquids: such as drinking water
- gases: such as steam that rises from boiling water.

Changing states

How do you get an ice cube to change into liquid water? You add **heat**, of course. Temperature is a kind of force that can cause an element or compound to change from one state to another. When an ice cube is in a freezer, it remains a solid. The freezer is very cold, so no heat is being added to the ice. But if you remove the ice cube from the freezer, it will begin to melt. This is because the surroundings of the ice cube have a higher temperature. The heat causes the molecules of water to gain energy and move faster. When this happens, the water changes state from solid to liquid.

Measuring freezing, melting, and boiling

You just read about how water can change from one state to another, but did you know that all **matter** can change from one state to another? It is true. It may require very high temperatures to get some types of matter to melt or become a gas, but it is possible with all matter. All matter has certain points at which they freeze, melt, and boil. These are called the freezing point, melting point, and boiling point.

Each addition of heat creates a change in state

GASES

+ Heat

LIQUIDS

+ Heat

SOLIDS

When enough heat is added to a substance, it will change states.

When the water in this spring reaches a very high temperature it becomes a gas, which we call steam.

Heating and cooling

Matter changes states when energy is added by heating or energy is removed by cooling. Even though the matter changes state when energy is added, the substance doesn't actually change. The substance may look different, but water is still water whether it is frozen, liquid, or gas. State changes are always reversible. The water that is rising as gas from a hot pot of water can condense back into a liquid drop of water. If that liquid drop of water is placed into a freezer, it will become a solid ice cube. No matter what state the water is in, it is still water!

EXPERIMENT!

Let's try an experiment to prove that state changes really are reversible. We will also determine whether state changes affect the amount of a substance. Do you think that freezing or melting water causes some water to be lost or gained? Let's find out.

You will need:
- sealable baggie
- water
- freezer
- scale.

Directions:
1 Fill the baggie about half full with water and make sure it is sealed completely.
2 Use the scale to find the weight of the water-filled baggie. Record your result.
3 Put the baggie in the freezer and leave until frozen (overnight if possible).
4 Remove the baggie from the freezer and find the weight and record your result.
5 Leave the baggie at room temperature until the ice melts.
6 Weigh the baggie one last time and record your result.

Was the baggie heavier when the water was ice? Did the weight of the water change between your first and third measurement? Was the change reversible?

You can perform experiments to see a substance change states.

Can You Graph Temperature?

We learned that sometimes it is necessary to make several temperature measurements to be sure we are making fair and accurate measurements. Graphing the results of our measurements can be an easy way to visualize what we find. This can make figuring out what our measurements mean easier.

A cold desert?

You know that deserts have very high temperatures in the day, but did you know that deserts can be very cold at night? To the right is a graph of the temperature measured every two hours over a 24-hour period in the Sahara Desert.

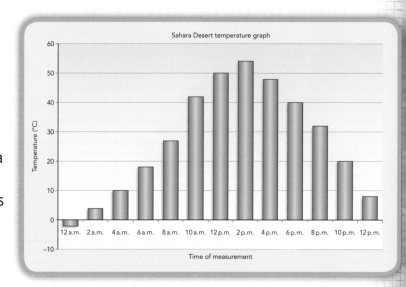

Putting the information into a bar graph makes it easier and more interesting to look at. The graph has one bar for every measurement made. The temperature (in Celsius) is listed on the vertical axis. This is known as the y-axis. The time the measurement was made is listed on the horizontal axis. This is known as the x-axis.

Try this at home!

Use what you have learned in this book to measure the temperature of your home. Try making measurements every 2 hours from the time you wake up until you go to bed. Put the information in a table as you make the measurements. When you are finished, you can put what you learned into a bar graph just like the one above.

Answers to You Do the Math

How Do We Measure Temperature? (page 9)

Plug the temperature we know into the formula: $°C = (136°F - 32) \times 5/9$.
Subtract: $136° - 32 = 104°$.
Multiply: $104° \times 5/9 = 57.78°$.
136°F is equal to 57.78°C!

Do the same to find degrees Fahrenheit: $°F = (-89.2°C \times 5/9) + 32$.
Multiply: $-89.2 \times 5/9 = -49.6$
Add: $-49.6 + 32 = -17.6$
-89.2°C is equal to -17.6°F!

What Is Used to Measure Temperature? (page 13)

41.4°C is rounded down to 41°C.

(page 15)

The average temperature on Mars is -25°C.

How Does Weather Affect Temperature? (page 21)

The inner ring is from the warmest year.

Glossary

Celsius (also known as centigrade) a temperature scale that registers the freezing point of water as 0° and the boiling point as 100°

climate change a change in the long-term weather patterns

degree a unit used to measure temperature

ectothermic an organism that regulates its body temperature by exchanging heat with its surroundings; cold-blooded

endothermic an organism that creates heat to maintain its body temperature, usually above the temperature of its surroundings; warm-blooded

equator imaginary circle around the Earth's surface; divides the Earth into hemispheres

Fahrenheit a temperature scale that registers the freezing point of water as 32° and the boiling point as 212°

global warming increase in Earth's average temperature

greenhouse gases any of the atmospheric gases that contribute to the greenhouse effect

heat a measure of the transfer of energy in matter

heat index measurement of the air temperature in relation to the humidity, used as an indicator of the perceived temperature

hemisphere half of the Earth divided by the equator

homeostasis ability of an organism to maintain a steady body temperature

humidity amount of water vapor present in the air

hyperthermia abnormally high body temperature

hypothermia abnormally low body temperature

matter what everything is made of

meteorologist one who reports and predicts weather conditions

prehistoric happening before written history

states of matter whether something is solid, liquid, or gas

temperature the degree of hot or cold of a body or environment. A measure of the energy of the particles in a sample of matter.

temperature record graph that shows the changes of temperature

thermal imaging a means to detect and translate temperature into visible images

thermometer instrument for measuring temperature

water vapor water in a gaseous state, especially when diffused as a vapor in the atmosphere and at a temperature below boiling point

wind chill factor a calculation of what a temperature feels like based on the actual temperature and wind speed

Find Out More

Books

Rodgers, Alan, and Streluk, Angella. *Measuring the Weather: Temperature*. Chicago: Heinemann Library, 2007.

Sullivan, Navin. *Temperature*. New York: Marshall Cavendish Benchmark, 2007.

Woodford, Chris. *Temperature*. Farmington Hills, Mich.: Blackbirch Press, 2005.

Websites

Weather Wiz Kids
http://www.weatherwizkids.com/weather-temperature.htm
Check out this site to learn more about temperature and use the conversion calculator.

EdHeads
http://www.edheads.org/activities/weather/
This colorful website offers lots of activities to learn more about weather.

Pew Center Climate Change Kids' Page
http://www.pewclimate.org/global-warming-basics/kidspage.cfm
Look at this website to answer questions about global warming and climate change.

Index